# How to Stand Out Online

## Simple Techniques to be Found Online Using Social Media and the Web

I0473838

## J. Bruce Jones

BruceJonesPublishing.com

**Notice of Liability:**
The information in this book is distributed on an "as is" basis, without warranty. While every precaution has been taken in the preparation of this book, neither the author no Bruce Jones Design Inc., shall have any liability to any person or entity with respect to any liability, loss, or damage caused or alleged to be caused directly or indirectly by the information or websites contained in this book.

**Trademarks:**
Throughout this book, trademarked names are used. Rather than put a trademark symbol in every occourrence of a trademarked name, we are using the names only in an editorial fashion and to the benefit of the trademark owner, with no intention of infringement of the trademark. Where those designations appear in this book, the designations have been printed in initial caps.

**Websites and Ideas:**
The Internet is a fluid changing medium and websites change all the time. All links are for information purposes only and are not warranted for content, accuracy or any other implied or explicit purpose.

The ideas express in this book are my own and there are no guarantees that you will have success with them. This book is intended to be informational and is my opinion only.

Published by Bruce Jones Design Inc
661 Washington Street, Norwood, MA 02062
781-255-7171

# Table of Contents

# The Bottom Line

**First:** Cultivating visibility on line is a process of putting yourself and your content out on a variety of platforms with a variety of active and passive techniques that get you in front of the people and organizations that need to know about you. The content must be original. It must matter to your readers, with all the i's dotted and the t's crossed and it must be accessible to the search engines with clear links back to you, your business or organization.

To be successful, this process takes constant and consistent effort across many different platforms over a long period of time. You must also be able to measure the content and know where you are starting from, what is happening and then adjust, and do again.

**Second:** It is essential to build market leadership and connections to the leaders and organizations in your market. The goal is to go from following the market to leading the market and becoming an authority in it.

**Third:** One of the results of the first two stages is that you develop exposure, products and services that you can promote and sell in your market.
We live in an amazing time; For almost no cost at all, we can spread our message around the globe.  Everyone, from the biggest companies to the smallest one man businesses, gets access to the same pieces of real estate, the same basic web page, video sites or social media platforms to send out their messages. What we do with it is up to us and how hard and smart we want to work, but we all can do it.

# Chapter 1
# The Basics

**To get started I recommend setting up 5 essential platforms.**
1. Gmail / Google account
2. Linkedin Account, personal and business
3. Facebook Page / Google+ Account
4. YouTube Channel
5. Some kind of blog or web presence

Keep an eye on Google+, it will become a major player

**These are also very valuable**
Twitter.com
Flicker.com / Picasa.com - photo sharing sites. Picasa is the
   photo end of Google+
Yelp.com, FourSquare.com, QR Codes, Pinterest.com
Wikipedia.com

**Productivity Sites That Are Very Helpful**
Evernote.com
Instapaper.com
Dropbox.com
Posterous.com

By next year, half of all cell phones will be smart phones and how you appear in a mobile world is going to become more and more important.

Along with the 5 essential platforms I also recommend setting up or being familiar with some additional Google tools.

A gmail account opens you to all Google products. Bing is increasingly popular and Yahoo survives but Google still rules. You will need to become familiar with or get ready to use some of these key Google products.

**Blogger**: We will need to set up a basic blog as a home

**Google+** account

**Google Alerts:** for watching our markets

**Google Analytics:** for tracking the visitors to our blog. It's very important to know what is going on.

**Google Reader**: very helpful for managing all of the information we will be following

**Google Keyword Tool External**: for analyzing our markets, figuring out keywords, ideas, writing copy

**Google Places:** letting the world know we exist

**Google Profile:** works with Google+. It's how Google sees you

**Google Trends:** what is going on, trends, Technority, Alltop.com

**Google Docs:** great place to organize our content online

**YouTube:** for showcasing our videos

Note: Google is currently going through some major changes with the release of Google+ and changes in how it is treating and ranking websites. The traditional ranking of quality backlinks is dropping and original, quality content and authorship are rising; all great things for those of us who create original content.

## Keys to Being Found On-line

- **First Key:** I believe that one of the main keys to exposure on line and to becoming known is to be producing and posting a variety of quality content in many, many different places in many different modes; text, video, images, pdf, etc. This process has to be done on a continual, regular basis; You can't just put something up and forget about it. You must constantly work at it. Working with an editorial calendar can really help.

- **Second Key** is that there must be clear paths for the reader to reach you. It is this second point that I think a lot of people fall down on and lose whatever they might have gained from their content.

- **Third Key** and maybe the most important is, just do it. Just start putting content out however you can. We have learned from working with many clients that this is one of the main reasons nothing is happening. You just have to try. Yhere is no clear path with social medial. It is completely the Wild West. But for so many people **Perfection Freezes Progress**. They are all waiting to get it right. Instead you need to fail, fail, fail, and then fix, fix, fix. Start small and learn and grow, but start.

- **Fourth Key Factor**, and this is pretty simple–is that everyone needs to fill in all of the boxes that are given to you in the account set up and in the profiles of every platform that you use. I know this sounds a little odd but the Profiles and About pages on websites, social media platforms and blogs are some of the most important sections in letting the world know who you are. Google often references this information. Google likes to see that the information is the same across different platforms. Make sure you spell your name the same way, the same company names, the same data.

Filling in the boxes also applies to blog posts, images that are being uploaded, videos that are being produced, tags that are being added, and everything else. Most sites give you many different ways to let the world know who you are. Most people don't seem to use them. These are all paths that lead viewers back to your main web home. Every social media platform lets you put in a web address, often an email address, and lots of descriptive copy about you and what you do. They all have areas to describe the content you are putting up and add web links back to your home.

Sites such as Flickr, YouTube and Linkedin, are built with this profile information in mind. Most people don't take advantage of it. It is very important for people to be able to reach you. Your content maybe working but if no one can reach you, it doesn't do you any good.

## Your Web Home

**What is a web home**? One of the theories on how to gain exposure is that you build a wagon wheel type of structure on the web. To be effective, you establish a hub or home base and then you have many different spokes or kinds of places from which you distribute content that feed or directs viewers back to your base. These can be videos, Twitter posts, other blogs, Flickr images, Hubpages, Facebook, Linkedin, Google+, or comments that you make on forums and blogs. Everything feeds back to one central place. People find you many different ways, on many different platforms; all of them help you to found. Along with being in all these places you also need to have clear channels of communication back.

I break down the social media platforms into two areas; ones that are **active** and are used on a regular basis to promote our business and ourselves and then some that are passive. The **passive** ones hold content on a permanent basis and are set up to help feed viewers back to our main web site or blog. Passive sites are like portfolios, holding our content and waiting for a viewer. We can also reference and cross-link a lot between the active and passive sites.

There are hundreds if not thousands of social media, video, and blogging sites on line, with more coming every day. For this article I am focusing on just the major or most popular ones. These are the sites that are in the news and are setting the standards. On the web, though, nothing lasts very long and new sites are coming online everyday so we need to constantly pay attention. And each industry has sites that are specific just to it and those too need to be identified.

## Active Promotion Sites

Active promotional sites are sites on which you add content on a regular basis, including your own blog, Linkedin, Facebook, Google+ and Twitter. Google and people who follow you like to see new, interesting and relevant content put up on a regular basis. If you are writing interesting material, people and Google will start to follow and look forward to the next release.

**Why a blog instead of a website?** I like blogs because when you are beginning, you don't know where you are going. Blogs allow you to assemble all kinds of content in one place: text, video, images, widgets, comments, social media connections. This is where you tell your story, develop your content, post your newest projects. You can easily make mistakes and learn and get your feet wet. For most people blogs work just fine for a web site, and you often don't need a web expert to establish.

Web sites are more permanent and developing them can take a lot more work. Usually when you set up a website you want to have a good idea of what you need and what you want to do on it. This is often not something you know when starting out. When you start out on the web the goal is not to get hung up on any one approach, but to get yourself out and learn as much as you can. Trying to put up a web site when you are beginning is a great way to get frozen. Blogs are great, you can literally put one up in about 5 minutes. You will know when you need a web site but in the beginning it isn't necessary.

Your blog will become your web home. All of the social media elements will link back to it and link out from there as well.

I recommend that you have several pages for your blog: a main blog page where all the posting is done, an About page, a Resource page, maybe a Portfolio page, a Product page, a Work with Me page and a Contact page.

Mix up the media on your blog: have text, videos, images, polls. Open your blog to comments. It all begins here.

**The Main Blog Platforms Are:**
- Google's Blogger, many large blogs often use one of the platforms listed below, but I really like Blogger for its ease of use and flexibility. Blogger.com

- WordPress.com and WordPress.org, .com is the free one, .org is the paid version. The blog software is free but it needs to be hosted on a host of your choosing. Hostgator.com is excellent. There are tons of free themes to choose from and also others that ae very affordable and offer a few more features.

- Tumblr.com

- Posterous.com

- MovableType.com free and paid

- LiveJournal.com

- Drupal.com

- Typepad.com

A key thing to remember when picking a place for a web home is that you should be able to easily add text, images and video whenever you want. You don't want to have to deal with a web master. You just want to be able to update and add content yourself.


**Linkedin.com**

Every professional should have a Linkedin page. This is your online profile or resume. You can connect with other professionals, list your accomplishments, the books you read, and the projects you work on. Google treats Linkedin very high in terms of authority. Search in Google for yourself and you will often see your Linkedin profile on page one of the results.

**Linkedin Status Box:** Many people use Linkedin for job hunting and sales leads. You can search for people and connections. You can also turn it around and use it for promotion. One of the great features of Linkedin is the status box. Once a week Linkedin sends out an update of what you have been doing from the status box, or any of the other sections you might have updated, to all of your contacts. What is nice about this is that you only have to fill this in once a week. A great time to do this is when you get the weekly update, usually on Thursday. People read this and are aware of the kinds of things you are doing. I write this status in a fly-on-the-wall style. I am not trying to be promotional, I am just trying to tell the story of my week, a new type of client I just landed, a conference I went to, or an interesting article I just read.

Linkedin also has connections to many of the major social media platforms like Twitter and Slideshare and is adding more all the time. Accept those Linkedin invites. People who are on Linkedin like being connected to others, so connect when asked. You will also note that if you search in Google on a person, it is their Linkedin profile is what will often show up on the first page of results. This is your image to the world, very powerful.

Take a look at mine as a good example of what you can do. Linkedin.com/in/brucejonesdesign

**Facebook.com**

Facebook is the 900lb gorilla in the room. It now has more than 800 million connected people and businesses. Facebook is all about community, personal and professional. For many people, Facebook is the web. The majority of their time is spent inside of Facebook. The average time spent on a website is maybe10 seconds; Facebook is an hour. Half of all Facebook users go to the site every day.

There are two basic kinds of pages, Personal pages and Places or Fan page. Places pages are pages for businesses or groups. Personal pages are for personal stuff, your friends, your connections. You are not supposed to be promotional or sell on these pages. You can talk about what you do and your experiences but it must be friendly. Places pages can be promotional. You can set up stores, sell stuff, promote sales, use coupons. We are only at the beginning of utilizing what can be done here.

Facebook is about community, connecting with your friends and fans. It is also a great place to highlight your images and videos. Places pages are searchable from Google, and for many business Facebook is becoming a great place for advertising. It is built for advertising, especially since they added the Like Buttons. The advertising tools are very powerful and it is very easy to focus on a narrow niche.

Facebook Places pages work great for businesses that have continual repeat customers, such as a yoga studio, spa or restaurant, business that need to sell open time slots. I am somewhat on the fence about businesses that deal with customers who rarely visit your office such as in an office building or who do project work. But if you are selling the same items over and over to the same customers on a regular basis such as a resturant, spa or classes, it can be very powerful. I have also seen some very effective uses of Facebook from a customer service point of view for businesses that need to communicate updates, status changes or build community.

**Twitter.com**

What is Twitter? Boy, that is a question that must be asked 1,000 times a day. Twitter is what is called a microblogging service. It lets people send and read small messages called tweets. The tweets are text based posts of up to 140 characters. You can send text, web site addresses, images and videos. Messages range from pointless babble to conversations, promotion, spam, and news. You can follow people and they can follow you.

Twitter is the social pulse of the web; usually meaning nothing and then meaning everything. If you have an event scheduled you can set up a hash tag for it and people can follow along. Twitter is a powerful tool to follow trends as they happen. You can search for who is leading a conversation. You can focus on your top 20.

These tools can also be turned around and used by businesses to gather customer feedback and to be sounding boards for issues. Invite your customers to comment on how you are doing or problems they might have, they. Twitter allows for very fast response to good and bad. Need a little help managing your followers check out applications like TweetDeck.com from Twitter.

**Google+**

Google+ is Google's effort to develop a social media platform like Facebook and Linkedin. Up to this point, they haven't been very successful at other attempts to build a social media platform, but Google+ might change all that. Google is constantly making changes to their search platform and Google+, adding Plus1 buttons, updating Blogger, Picassa, YouTube and many other things.

A very interesting feature in Google+ is their Circles and the Hangout feature. Circles are the way that they allow you to organize your friends and connections. When you make a post, you select which circles and which set of connections will be able to see it. This allows you to tailor your content to those with whom you want to connect. No more marketing stuff to your family. Hangout allows you to have video conference calls, both private and public, with the camera built into your computer. Setting up a Hangout takes two seconds and it is free. All kinds of connections are possible.

Because this is Google, we have to take Google+ seriously. I recommend joining and let's see where it goes.

**What Do I Write About?**

Write about your life, your projects, drop in interesting articles that you come across, interesting videos, pictures of your products, your projects, your people.

If I had to pick just one or two places to be, for professionals it would be a blog and Linkedin. If I owned a retail establishment of some kind, it might be a blog and Facebook.

# Passive Promotional Sites

Passive sites are sites that you load with content and they sit out there working for you, such as Youtube, Flickr, Picasa, Scribd, Hubpages, and Squidoo. All of these sites have the ability to build community and have interaction but mostly they are passive. You aren't usually on them everyday, but they are very powerful in building your brand and distributing your content.

The same thing applies here as on the active sites. You have the ability to add profile and descriptive copy to help promote yourself and your content. These sites work if people can find what you have put up. This is usually done by filling in all the profile and item boxes with descriptive and accurate copy. What is interesting is that most people don't do this, so if you do, you really stand out. Getting your content found on Google is often a challenge. Getting it found on YouTube or some of these site is much easier.

**YouTube.com**
YouTube is the world's largest video hosting site, with 135 million people visiting everyday and over 3 billion searches every day. YouTube dominates all other video hosting sites. One of the stats that is amazing about YouTube is that if you have just 2 videos on YouTube you are 52x more likely to be found in Google search.

There are several genius moves that have propelled YouTube to the front. One, they can take almost any form of video produced. If you can upload it, it plays. They have taken away most of the technical issues. The second great move is the ability to share your video anywhere you want. They give you the embed code, which you copy and paste on your blog, website or Facebook. This is one of the essences of social media; the ability to share. And the third important factor is the ability to drop in large amounts of descriptive content and web links. This last point is key because this is how Google works and finds your content; it searches on words.

YouTube is also making major changes; it has a new design, a new interest in videos that are part of a series, new original content and a new direction in becoming more of a social media site. In reality YouTube is trying to move away from being so passive, they are looking for view activity and community.

**Keys to Getting Found on YouTube**

- A good descriptive title this is key. Make it descriptive and accurately describe what your video is about.

- Below the video, add good descriptions with full http web addresses connected back to your web home. You can add very large amounts of text in YouTube. Put the full web address first and then the descriptive copy. You can also add additional web links here. Google searches text, not pictures or video, so put in as many words as you can. Can't think of what to write, how about a transcript of the video.

- Good relevant tags or keywords, you can add up to 483 characters. Remember to include your name.

- Videos that have social activity and lots of viewer comments.

What is amazing is most people don't do these things. Getting found in Google is a challenge. Getting found in YouTube is not hard at all. Anything you want to know is on YouTube. It is where you want to be first. Then move to other video sites. Remember, Google owns YouTube and really likes it and YouTube is a global platform and overseas viewers have money too.

## What Kind of Videos Should I Put Up?

- How-to and tutorial videos work very well
- Testimonials
- Interviews with experts and people from your company
- Product descriptions, reviews and demonstrations
- (FAQ) Frequently asked questions
- Customer responses
- Ask views to sign up for your newsletter or something else
- Lessons
- News about your organization
- Then all the crazy stuff, often involving a cat

Keep them short, add contact info, calls to action and lots of good descriptive copy and keywords

**Flickr.com and Picasa.com**

Flickr and Picasa are photo sharing sites. Flickr is part of Yahoo and Picasa is part of Google. In fact Picasa is now the photo end of Google+. Both of these sites allow you to upload, describe, tag and drop in web links. Viewers can search through all of the images. If your name and web address is on them, maybe they can find you. Images of all kinds are huge on-line and in Google. Take a look at Google Images and search on your market. Are your images showing up there? Lots of others are.

**Scribd.com, Slideshare.com**

Scribd is like YouTube but for pdf files. It is the world largest social reading and publishing company and is filled with publications, reports, books and all kinds of documents that you can read on line, download and in some cases charge for. Like the others, you can describe, tag and link any of the documents. Because these are pdf files, they are searchable in Google. Scribd.com is a great place to upload a story or article and see if it gets found.

Slideshare.com is a service that allows you to upload and share PowerPoint and pdf presentations. Slideshare works with some of the major social media platforms including Linkedin.com.

**HubPages.com, Squidoo.com, Microblogs**

These are small generally single-topic websites that are designed around sharing advertising revenue for user-generated articles and other content. In my experience HubPages.com is one of the best lead generating sites.

To sum up, the first key with all of this is to produce content or take existing content and spread it around the web on a variety of platforms. This content should be original, interesting, helpful, and released on a continual and consistent basis. You don't have to create mountains of it but it should all be yours. The second key is that there should be clear connections back to your website and to you. This is done using the profiles, and in the content itself. And the third key to remember that it takes time. This isn't going to happen overnight but it will happen if you keep at it.

# Chapter 2
# Top 20 Technique, Establishing Market Leadership and Getting Noticed

In chapter 2 we focus on some current writings by Internet marketers Ed Dale, Hugh MacLeod and others.

To be noticed and to be located on the web, you need to be out in the world with something important to say. The top people in your industry, the people that hold market leadership, are there because they talk about things that matter to you. You want to follow and learn from them.

The Top 20 can be marketleaders or they can be people or organizations you would like to be connected to and noticed by.

The task here is to put together a list of your Top 20, As Ed says, "the depth of your market leadership, is directly related to how high up the "food chain" you are. The higher up the food chain, the more likely they are talking about you." Are any of these people following you?

"Who's reading your stuff? Who is following you on Twitter?"

If nobody is following you, you need to get on their radar. The easiest way to get on their radar is to produce great content that speaks to their market. A key thing to remember and not go crazy over is that not everything you produce will be great. Some will be crappy. Some will be. And some will change the world. You don't know which piece of content that is, but if you don't start putting out quality content you will never find out. Start putting out content and see what happens. Watch, adjust, learn and keep going. Google Analytics is very helpful in this area, as is social media. That is one of the main reasons for using it.

**First thing is to identify** the Top 20 movers and shakers in your market. Write them down. Don't know 20. Identify those you can, and then go to sites like Twitter and Twitter Search to see who shows up in your market. Go to the blogs you follow. Who are they talking about? Who is writing the articles? Go to Amazon and see who is writing books on these topics. Search on Google and see who shows up.

**Second, to be noticed** by these people, you need to be where they are and see how they communicate with the world. If they are blogging then you need to be blogging. If they are using video, then you use video to talk about what matters. You want to be in their space, using their tools.

**Third, tracking.** You need to keep up with your market leaders. You need to know what they are doing and saying. Twitter is a great way to do this. If they are on Twitter, you can create a list of just these people using the List feature. When you follow someone, they will often follow you. They most likely aren't paying attention to you, but they will follow. Linkedin is a great way to link with them. The Linkedin weekly Status box will become a vital connection tool for this. You can also follow them using Google Alerts, connect their RSS feeds to Google Reader to make it easier to keep up with them, connect with Facebook. Put them in your Google+ circles.

**Fourth, interact.** This is the connection part. This isn't stalking. This isn't pestering them with requests. It is being in their space and contributing to it. A key tip from Ed is "Never ask for anything! Even more importantly, never be needy!" It is more about how can I help? How can I serve? Help with requests, give constructive feedback, comment and contribute.

**And the last step, start creating content** that matters to your market and do it on a consistent, dependable basis. If you are helping and contributing in your market and community, you might eventually be seen as one of the Top 20.

An important point here is to be patient; this doesn't happen over night, it may take you several years to establish your platform.

# Chapter 3
# Making Money

Along with getting found, which is our primary goal, we can also use these skills to make money. In this third part I will talk a little about doing this.

We use all these platforms to host our content, tell our story and bring readers back to our site or into our sales funnel. As a result of all this effort, we can build our business, organizations and services. And we can make money. Some of this money can also be made from the content that we put up to promote ourselves.

Pat Flynn from the Smart Passive Income blog is a master at doing and at explaining this. I would recommend checking out his blog smartpassiveincome.com/ when you get a chance.

Blogs are a fantastic place to assemble and test content and to get feedback to see if anyone is interested. You can tell very quickly what people are interested in.

You can start with a very rough idea for a book or a DVD/film or products like t-shirts and hats. Let's say you have an antique business and want to write a book about the development of chairs in America. You start by posting photographs on your blog of different period chairs and drop in good descriptive text. Then watch your comments, your blog stats and your Google Analytics data to see what readers are interested in.

Google Analytics is the idea tool for seeing if anyone cares, see what they read and what keywords they used to find your website, it is amazing. If nothing happens in response to your post or blog, try tables. If something happens, write more on chairs, put a video up on YouTube and drop it into your blog, put images on Flickr. All of these platforms have stats and give you feedback on what viewers are looking at. You don't have to build your book from beginning to end. You don't have to do much at all. Just keep assembling content on the blog. Once you have enough material and you know what people are interested in, you can copy it off and assemble it into a book or a film or a course.

Remember also that you can build a mailing list of interested people who come to your site. AWeber.com is a great service for doing this. Give away an early chapter in exchange for an email address. Ask for feedback on your posts; say "I am thinking of pulling this material together for a book or DVD. Is anyone interested?" Surveys can also be very helpful for figuring out what readers are interested in. Check out SurveyMonkey.com, they have a free survey feature if you stay with ten questions or less. As you work on designs or layout, you can ask your readers questions like "Do you like the page to look like this or like that? What kind of additional information would you like me to include?" Crowd source and engage your readers in the process, build fans, sell your products back to them.

*Note: There is no guarantee that you will make money online using these ideas and techniques. Your earning potential is entirely dependent upon you, and the then current state of web marketing at the time you employ such techniques and ideas. It is entirely dependent upon your skills, resources, marketing knowledge and the time you devote to the effort.*

## Some Money Making Ideas

If you can make videos, always be shooting. If you write, always be writing. Maybe you are somewhere on a trip or doing a story; why not shoot a travel video or write a story about your experiences while you are there, or an expanded version of the making of your story that you can sell on DVD? Produce something based off the location. Maybe shoot and sell stock video and images. All of the major stock photo houses now take video along with images. (Remember the tripod. They are very picky about this.) You can also sell stock footage yourself. You can write about your experience and make a book.

Bring a still camera with you and shoot photos for a book, "Bugs of the Jungle." With print on demand these days there is no need for a publisher. You can do this yourself. On services like CreateSpace.com from Amazon.com and Lulu.com you can host and display your book, they take care of the selling, production and delivery. Afterwards, they just send you the check. You can promote your products with the same website marketing network you have built to promote yourself.

## Some Possible Product Ideas

All of these ideas can be produced for free or very little cost outside of a little knowledge and your labor.

- **Ebooks, and real books.** Sell the book on Amazon. Give away the ebook as a bonus. "Send me your receipt I will send you a free pdf".

- Adult books, kid books, instructional how to books, online magazines

- **Stock photo and stock video**

- **Audio programs.** Remember every video has an audio track that can be pulled off, turned into an mp3 for an iPod, or just a narrated tour of the experience

- **Run a webinar** with GoToMeeting.

- How about a **paid teleseminar** on your experiences. Services like FreeConferenceCall.com are great resources for running and recording a telephone interview. And I understand that Skype is coming to Facebook shortly. Talk to small groups about your experiences. Charge for it. Google+ has the Hangout feature for up to 10 active participants and many more in just listening mode. Teach a class or consult over the web, run a Meetup. Record it using a screen capture program such as Screenflow on the Mac or Captiva on the PC. Use it for promotion or a bonus gift.

- **DVDs of a trip.** Pull the different travel videos together into bigger a collection, CreateSpace has print-on-demand DVDs and streaming video. Combine the DVD with a book of images and you have now become a mini PBS Ken Burns.

- Hire out to **speak at live events**. Hold your own live event. Use a free service like UStreamTV.com and hold your own live event online. Once you have some followers, announce a live UStream.TV event, maybe charge for it but at the least record it.

- **Use YouTube to build an online web-based TV series**. Remember, we don't have to work in half hour or hour blocks anymore. Your        series can be 1 or 2 minutes long

- If you are a musician or a teacher, how about doing **live classes using Skype, UStream.TV or Google+ Hangout** with your students? This opens you up to teaching anywhere in the world. Announce a free event using Twitter and Facebook, and then during that event mention an upcoming special paid event. Your classes can all become online content to attract other students.

## Social Media Resources

**Books on Social Media**

- **Crush It! Cash in On Your Passion** by Gary Vaynerchuk. A great short, right-to-the-point read on building your own personal brand using social media. Personally recommended, especially chapters 6-10/

- **Social Media 101: Tactics and Tips to Develop Your Business Online** by Chris Brogan

- **Trust Agent** by Chris Brogan

- **Social Media Bible** by Lon Safko

- **Inbound Marketing: Get Found Using Google, Social Media and Blogs** by Brian Halligan, Dharmesh Shah, and David Meerman Scott. These are the HubSpot guys

- **ProBlogger** by Darren Rowse

- **The Constant Contact Guide to Email Marketing** by Eric Groves. This is an excellent book on setting up and managing an email system

**Thought Leaders to Follow**

- **Chris Brogan**. Subscribe to his Free Updates. Chris writes on being an online person, building a company, being in business, and marketing. Start subscribing and you will get it. ChrisBrogan.com

- **Seth Godin**. Seth is one of those marketers you want to pay attention to. He often takes an opposite view and makes you think. He has a daily news feed that is worth reading. Maybe not as polished on the day to day as Chris Brogan but I enjoy his writing a lot. He has written over 10 books and if you get a chance to see any of his videos on marketing they are well worth it. Search on YouTube. SethGodin.typepad.com/

- **Pat Flynn.** Pat is one of the most creative people when it comes to using a blog as a home for your efforts. He is very clear and shares all of his techniques with his readers. He has one of the best free ebooks that I have read on the process on how to make a book from a blog. You can download it for free at this blog. SmartPassiveIncome.com/

- **Ed Dale**. Ed is a master at Internet marketing and using all of the tools to build market leadership. I have followed him for a number of years and I am constantly learning from his leadership. Runs a free online marketing course at the end of the summer, The Challenge, that is well worth it. Teaches you pretty much everything you need to know. Free to sign up and follow.
  EdDale.co, and Challenge.co

- **Joan Stewart**. Joan is a small business PR specialist. She releases a simple, to-the-point newsletter every Tuesday with excellent tips on how to promote your business or self. PublicityHound.com/

- **Andy Jenkins**. Andy is the Video Boss, and an amazing marketer. His free content on Internet marketing and marketing with video is unmatched. AndyJenkinsBlog.com/

- **Gideon Shalwick**. Gideon is Andy Jenkins light, with excellent simple clear instructions on how to make and market your business using video GideonShalwick.com/

- **Social Media Examiner**. An excellent guide to social media with informative articles and resources. SocialMediaExaminer.com/

There are many others. Each industry has its leaders. Find out who they are and follow them.

# Sites to Watch

Every industry has news or information sites that tell you what is going on and what is new, such as in the social media space Mashable.com or in the blog world, Technorati.com/. Your job is to figure out what they are and subscribe to them.

You can find these sites by searching in Google Blogs or Google Forums. Watch and see who is commenting on sites in your markets and where they are hanging out. Many contributors drop in their credit lines next to a post to tell you how could you can connect with them and what sites they are on.

# Production Resources

### Publish a Book or DVD Using Print on Demand

- Lulu.com, various binding and cover options: Lulu.com/

- Blurb.com, great for photo and art books: Blurb.com

- Createspace.com/Amazon, Print on Demand site for books, DVD, CDs, this gets you in the Amazon system: CreateSpace.com

- Kindle Direct Publishing: kdp.amazon.com/self-publishing/signin

- Scribd pdf publishing site: Scribd.com/

**Make a Physical Product Using Print on Demand**

- CafePress, hundreds of available products: CafePress.com

- Zazzle, tshirts, mugs, hats, waterbottles: Zazzle.com

**Video Distribution / Sharing Sites**

- YouTube video hosting: YouTube.com

- Blip.tv, loves series: Blip.tv/

- Vimeo.com, HD quality: Vimeo.com/

- UStream.tv, live streaming: UStream.tv/

- DailyMotion, YouTube of Europe: DailyMotion.com/us

- Traffic Geyser, video distribution site: TrafficGeyser.com

**Email Hosting and Marketing Sites**

- Constant Contact, well respected in the corporate world: ConstantContact.com

- AWeber, a favorite of Internet marketers: Aweber.com

- Mail Chimp: MailChimp.com/

- My Emma: MyEmma.com/

- iContact, has a free edition for small business, individuals, and local organizations: iContyacty.com
- Survey Monkey for surveys: SurveyMonkey.com

## About the Author: J. Bruce Jones

J. Bruce Jones is a Massachusetts based business graphic designer, software developer, musician, author and independent video producer. Bruce is the author of over 14 books and writes on various topics including: playing and learning music with his Essential Chord books, and guides to getting found on YouTube, using Google Analytics, and general thoughts on business and marketing.

Bruce is the developer of the World of Maps editable clip art map collection for PowerPoint and Adobe Illustrator for presentations, illustrations, graphic design, and websites, distributed through various websites including; www.mapsfordesign.com, www.bjdesign.com and Amazon. He is also the developer of Antique and Historical Maps, a collection of royalty free, antique digital maps from 1500s to the 1900s, used for graphic design, illustration, web sites and education.

Bruce is very active in both producing and creating original programming for local public access television and the web and also for businesses interested in promoting themselves using video over services like YouTube and UStream.tv.

Bruce is a contributor to the Bill Gentile Backpack Journalism Workshops, along with various consulting and lecturing.

Connect with me on Linkedin: Linkedin.com/in/brucejonesdesign
Connect with me on Twitter: Twitter.com/bjdesign

**Bruce's Web Sites**

Graphic Design and Marketing

BruceJonesDesign.com

RapidEbookPublishing.com

BruceJonesDesign.blogspot.com

MakeMarketPublishYourBook.com

**World of Maps Editable Clip Art sites**

BJDesign.com

MapsforDesign.com

FreeUSandWorldMaps.com

**Music Sites**

AcousticMusicTV.com

AcousticMusicTV.blogspot.com

**Books**

Essential Chords for Guitar, Mandolin, Ukulele and Banjo

Left Hand Chords for Guitar, Mandolin, Ukulele and Banjo

Blank Sheet Music for Guitar, Mandolin

A series of books for geography and education on World Maps, USA and State Maps and World Regional Maps

Vote 2012 Presidential Election Coloring Book

My First ABC and Number Coloring Book

www.ingramcontent.com/pod-product-compliance
Lightning Source LLC
Chambersburg PA
CBHW071555170526
45166CB00004B/1683